# GREEN IGUANAS

R. D. Bartlett
Patricia P. Bartlett

BARRON'S

*All inquiries should be addressed to:*
Barron's Educational Series, Inc.
250 Wireless Boulevard
Hauppauge, New York 11788
http://www.barronseduc.com

*Library of Congress Catalog Card No. 99-29656*

International Standard Book No. 0-7641-1126-4

**Library of Congress Cataloging-in-Publication Data**

Bartlett, Richard D., 1938–
    Green iguanas / R. D. Bartlett and Patricia P. Bartlett.
        p.   cm.  — (Reptile keeper's guides)
    ISBN 0-7641-1126-4
    1. Green iguanas as pets.  I. Bartlett, Patricia Pope, 1949–
II. Title.  III. Series: Bartlett, Richard D., 1938– Reptile keeper's guides.
SF459.I38B365  1999
639.3'95—dc21                                               99-29656
                                                                  CIP

Printed in Hong Kong
987654321

# Contents

# Preface

This book is designed to help you with the care of one of today's most popular pet lizards, the great green iguana. It includes husbandry and updated dietary information for these neotropical herbivores. With the knowledge gained by many researchers and hobbyists over the past 30 years, these once difficult-to-keep lizards can live 15 years in your care. Although they can become tame, they can also be "moody" and difficult. The large size of an iguana when adult dictates a cage of comparable size, and if you tire of the lizard, finding a suitable foster home may be challenging. Because a very high percentage of the green iguanas now available in the American pet trade are farmed or bred in captivity, your choice of a pet green iguana will not mean that one is taken directly from the wild. We hope that you will enjoy your iguana, and that the information we have provided will make it just a little easier to understand your magnificent lizard.

This brightly colored baby iguana was hatched on a Colombian iguana ranch.

# Introduction

In the mid-1960s, pet iguanas were comparative newcomers to the pet market. Then, as now, potential owners were fascinated by these miniature green "dragons" that could reach adult sizes of almost 6 feet! Prices were certainly low enough—who could resist a bright-eyed hatchling that sold for $2.95? We had pet iguanas, but we lacked husbandry knowledge. Dietary guidelines were limited and, by today's standards, woefully lacking. Very, very few iguanas reached their adult size, and as a result, few owners were faced with the problem of housing and feeding a big lizard.

Both the iguanas and their owners have much greater potential for success today. Field observations have told us the basics—at least what we *think* are the basics—of social behaviors and feeding choices. Research by dedicated hobbyists and veterinarian/herpetologists has brought us information about what plants and vegetables to feed, caging guidelines, health maintenance, and breeding techniques. Longevity of a well-cared-for iguana is now 15 years or more. Feral populations are now established in warm climates in several areas of the United States, probably the result of released captives. Vacationers in southern Florida can view green iguanas in the wild. With a better understanding of green iguana behavior and requirements, hobbyists can make better decisions concerning their long-lived pets.

This alert look was caused by an approaching dog.

# What Is a Green Iguana?

The great green iguana, *Iguana iguana*, a popular pet species, ranges widely through much of tropical Latin America and on a few of the islands of the Lesser Antilles. The green iguana has one close relative, the Antillean green iguana, *Iguana delicatissima,* from islands in the Antillean chain.

Because it is protected, no legal specimens of the Antillean iguana are available in the pet trade. In contrast, green iguanas are a very common pet store lizard. Probably because of released pet iguanas, feral populations now exist on Hawaii, in extreme southern Florida, and in Cameron County, Texas, in the lower Rio Grande Valley. Between 800,000 and 1,000,000 green iguanas are imported for the pet trade each year. Most are commercially raised in Latin America just for this market.

Green iguanas are native to much of Latin America.

In the wild, green iguanas are arboreal lizards that claim high trees near waterways. In addition to the warming benefits of sunshine, the trees also offer distinct vantage points. The better an iguana can view the world around it (with all its possible food sources, potential predators, and potential mates), the better off it is.

Green iguanas are also superb swimmers. If danger threatens, iguanas simply dive into the water and swim to safety, using their long tails as both propellers and rudders. They may stay submerged until the perceived danger has passed.

Although a large male iguana or even a large female iguana may have few enemies (the tail is a very effective weapon, and iguanas don't hesitate to bite or rake with their claws to defend themselves), getting to adult size means avoiding predators. Young iguanas are food for anything that can catch them, and the hatchlings are essentially bite-sized. Brown basilisks, ctenosaurs (large spiny-tailed iguanas), and several species of snakes feed upon iguanas, and tree-dwelling predators such as monkeys, coatimundis, hawks, and jays are adept at the

A feral green iguana partakes of the afternoon sunshine in Miami.

The Antillean green iguana is the closest relative of the great green iguana.

grab-and-consume method of iguana capture. In South and Central America, humans hunt and consume iguanas and their eggs or capture the females for sale to one of the iguana ranches that supply the pet trade.

The great green iguana has several very distinctive identifying characteristics. Below the tympanum (external eardrum) are from one to several grossly enlarged, rounded scales. (The Antillean iguanas lack these, which is an easy way to distinguish between the species, should you need to.) Some green iguanas from Mexico and northern Central America bear pronounced elongated scales on the snout. At one time, these lizards were classified as the now invalid subspecies, *Iguana rhinolopha*.

Along the underside of the thighs, green iguanas have a series of pores called femoral pores. Best developed in the males, these pores secrete a waxy gray substance. The exudate from the femoral pores contains scenting molecules called pheromones, which are used to mark territory. Both males and females have vertebral crests, a row of enlarged, pointed scales along the spine, beginning at the head and decreasing in size down to the tail. The crest is larger and more pronounced in the males and makes them look larger to their opponents and to potential mates.

All green iguanas bear a dewlap, a fold of skin under the throat, which is displayed in courtship and territorial behaviors. Generally speaking, the males do most of the territorial displays, but the females also display. Adult males are larger, have heavier jowls and swollen temporal areas, and are brighter in overall coloration than females.

On the top of the head, between and posterior to the eyes, is a small grayish organ that looks like a modified scale. This is the parietal eye, which is sensitive to light and dark cycles (photoperiod) and so aids in the timing of the breeding cycle. The parietal eye bears a vestigial lens and a retina and transmits its messages to the pineal body in the brain by a nerve.

A subadult male green iguana basks in a tangle of vegetation.

A portrait of an adult male great green iguana.

# The Green Iguana as a Pet

When you select your pet iguana, you want to consider two factors. You want a healthy iguana, and you want one that seems tameable. With these factors on your side, you have a greater chance of enjoying your pet.

Choosing a healthy iguana is fairly simple. Healthy baby iguanas are green (vibrant and intense—like healthy leaves of a growing plant), blue green, or, rarely, a grayish green. An occasional iguana may also bear prominent, dark, vertical markings, with the markings near the shoulder and the hips the most prominent, but the bright green coloration is your indication of a healthy iguana.

Body weight is another health indicator. A healthy iguana has good body weight. Do not purchase one that looks thin, in the rib area or especially in the pelvic girdle. A healthy baby iguana should have bright eyes and watch the movements around it—your movements, for example. (Do not choose an iguana with dull, sunken

A baby green iguana sits atop a limb in a sunny window.

This healthy appearing baby green iguana is freshly imported.

Bright eyes and alert appearance are two indicators of green iguana health.

eyes and listless mien. It will probably not survive.)

The health of your animal will be directly related to the conditions under which it has been kept. Look for an iguana that has been kept in a clean cage with ample fresh drinking water, fresh food in the dish, and a warmed and well-illuminated basking area.

Attitude is almost as important as health. If among those alert, bright-eyed babies, there is one that stay calms when you reach in to gently grasp it, choose it. The more calm a baby iguana is, the easier and more fun it will be to tame it!

One minor point about choosing a hatchling iguana is that iguanas are impossible to sex at that small size. There are sexing services available, once you get your pet home and are certain that it's doing well. The services analyze the DNA you send them in the form of a tiny blood sample or a piece of shed skin.

Once you've chosen your new pet, get it home safely. If the outside tem-perature is under 70°F as you leave the store, shelter the box containing your iguana under your coat to avoid chilling the animal. If it's colder than 60°F, use a hot water bottle and a Styrofoam box. Release the animal in its cage, with the perching branches, basking lights, and food and water dishes already in place. Begin the taming process as soon as you want; in the above-average pet shop, the caring and well-trained store employees will have already begun working with the iguanas in their care, and the taming process will have already begun.

Do you have more than one iguana? Even though baby and subadult iguanas can be housed communally, adults are solitary lizards that defend their territories vigorously against incursions by other iguanas. The culminating interactions between two wild males can be particularly savage; those against females are

A baby green iguana warily surveys its domain.

usually less so. This is especially so if the female happens to be sexually receptive.

Two maturing male iguanas that have been housed together since baby-hood are very likely to become incompatible with age. Occasionally a male and a female will prove less antagonistic, but you need to be ready to provide separate housing if necessary. Fights can result in wounds of varying severity, which will need cleansing and occasionally veterinary treatment. Even with initial treatment, abscesses may result, again requiring veterinary assessment.

## Size Makes a Difference

There's a good reason for choosing a hatchling iguana over one that is 18 inches long or longer. Most subadult and adult iguanas are not good candidates for taming. If they are from the iguana farms or directly from the wild (and there's little difference between the two), their instinct tells them that people are dangerous. Actually, iguanas know that anything that isn't an iguana is bad news, and they know that you're no iguana.

Subadult to adult iguanas have more difficulty in adjusting to captivity, a new diet, and the presence and smell of humans and other animals. In addition, the larger the iguana is, the more difficult it is to physically handle. Calming and holding a writhing iguana after it has lashed you smartly across the face with its tail is a study in patience.

## Taming and Handling Your Iguana

The responses of an iguana to you and the environment you provide are entirely different from those of a domestic mammal or a pet bird. Some iguanas resist all overtures by their human keepers, never becoming tame. With much dedicated work on the part of their owners, other iguanas may become reasonably tame but resist handling. This means that such an iguana will remain calm as you approach its cage, will feed readily,

Speed impaired by winter cold, this iguana, held by Billy Griswold, could have been easily caught by any predator.

and may even take food from your fingers but not enjoy being picked up. Other iguanas become completely docile, and calmly move toward the cage front as the cage door is opened.

Until they are tamed, baby iguanas will require gentle restraint when being held.

When tame, baby iguanas are seldom reclusive.

A tame iguana may submit to wearing a harness and riding on its owner's hat or along the back of the car seat. It may enjoy being stroked on its neck. It is often given the range of its owner's home while its owner is home and will choose to rest near its owner when he or she watches TV or works at a desk.

It can take a concerted effort on your part to truly tame an iguana, and, even then, some iguanas have "bad days." The reason behind this resistance is simply many years of evolution.

By nature, iguanas are rather solitary creatures. This is especially true of males. It is the most dominant ones that have the greatest success in breeding. To assert dominance, they display, bite, and lash with their tails. In a real "knock down, drag-out" fight they may use their claws as well. Females are less dominant but have their own territorial tendencies. Survival instinct dictates that touched or grasped iguanas either flee or fight. It is this instinct that you must overcome.

Until your iguana is completely used to its new home and to you, always move very slowly. You will soon learn what your iguana will readily tolerate and what it is more reluctant to allow. Concentrate on overcoming the negative responses.

Remember that many iguanas will resist being grasped from above. If you wish to lift your iguana, approach it slowly from behind or induce it to step onto your hand or arm. For bigger iguanas, wear a long-sleeved thick shirt. Once it is clinging securely, restrain the iguana with your other hand (if necessary) to prevent it from falling or jumping. You will be able to move more quickly as your iguana becomes accustomed to this procedure. Always keep your iguana away from people's faces, even your own.

If your iguana refuses to allow you to touch it or to be held in your hand, try the same exercise with a thin stick wrapped with cloth at the tip. Some iguanas initially find this a more acceptable alternative than hand-touching. If your iguana will allow this, shorten the stick a little every 3 or 4 days until it is at last discarded and your hand is touching your iguana.

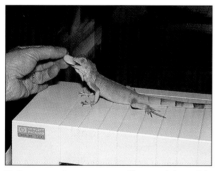

Baby green iguanas usually consider a bit of apple a welcome treat.

By following these suggestions, your iguana should soon become sufficiently used to your repetitive motions to allow increasing familiarity and more hurried movements on your part. Do remember that iguanas can be rather easily startled and may drop from your arm or shoulder and run away. An unrestrained iguana should never be taken out-of-doors.

## A Note About Color

To date, the only color morph developed in green iguanas is the albino. Albino iguanas have occasionally been offered for sale at specialty breeders or at expos such as the Captive Breeders' Expo in Orlando, Florida.

Hatchling albinos are so pale that they appear translucent. They soon become a chalk white and, when adult, vary from almost a pure white to a yellowish white. Upon the rare occasion when hatchling albinos are available, they command prices in the thousands of dollars each.

Some iguanas, like this large female, are very basically colored.

# Caging

Although it is fine to start with a small cage for your baby iguana, you must be prepared to provide progressively larger quarters as the iguana grows. Keep in mind that not only are iguanas active lizards but that some males can exceed a total length of 6 feet (females may reach 4.5 feet). Many of the more successful keepers and breeders of iguanas utilize an entire room, or room-sized cage, for their lizards.

For a hatchling, a cage the size of a 20-gallon tank (12 in. × 12 in. × 30 in.) will suffice. As a general rule, the width of your cage should be at least three fourths the total length of your iguana, the height should be about the length of your iguana, and the length of the cage should always be at least one and a half times the length of your iguana.

For the early part of your iguana's life, you can buy cages that are large enough. Within a few years, you'll need to make your iguana's cage, or you'll need to find someone who can do this for you.

Wood and wire are ideal materials for an outside iguana cage.

An adult iguana will need an illuminated/heated cage at least 4.5 feet wide, 6 feet high, and 8 or 9 feet long. In the Deep South, where temperatures are consistently warm and the humidity is high, large outdoor cages may be made for tame iguanas from smooth welded wire. Such cages may also be used during warm weather even at northern latitudes. An indoors, warm, draft-free cage will be needed for colder weather in the north, and this cage must also help provide the high humidity your iguana will need. You must always watch that your iguana does not injure its nose in efforts to escape and that the cage is devoid of snags and crevices in which the iguana may catch and injure a leg or tail.

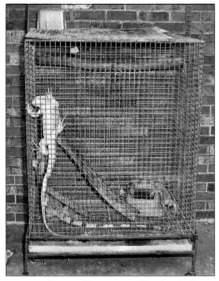

Iguanas in outside cages often bask from midmorning until dusk.

# Housing Options

## Cages

### Wood and Wire Caging

If your adult iguana will spend most of its life in a cage, you'll need to provide enough space for it to move around. This means a floor space of at least 8 feet × 10 feet and a height of at least 6 feet. If your iguana is allowed to wander through your house, the cage can be slightly smaller. Any cage should be provided with tree trunks and climbing limbs, elevated shelves, access to natural sunlight or a bank of ultraviolet-producing light, a hotspot for basking, areas of seclusion, a feeding bowl, and an adequate supply of clean water.

A simple cage begins with a framework of wooden 2 × 2s. The components of the frame are nailed or screwed together. Heavy wire staples,

Large, but easily moved outdoor cages of wood and wire are ideal for green iguanas during suitable weather.

the kind you hammer in, are used to fasten the wire mesh to the outside of the framework. The bottom can be a piece of plywood (3/4 in. is best, but 5/8 in. will do) or wire mesh if the cage sits atop a bed of newspaper.

Welded wire mesh of at least 1/2-inch squares is suggested for large iguanas. A smaller mesh is apt to catch the toenails of these large lizards and could cause injury to the toes. If a smooth welded mesh or a plastic covered wire is used, it will help prevent the lizard from abrading its nose as it explores its cage.

When you build the door, make it large enough so that you can reach to the bottom of the cage to clean it, or add another door near the bottom of the cage for this purpose.

Casters will allow you to move your cage easily, and the easier it is to move, the more likely you are to move the cage to a sunny window or outside if the weather permits. If you have an outside deck or porch, make the cage narrow to allow it to be moved in or out through the door—6 or 8 feet long by 2 inches narrower and 2 inches shorter than your exterior door will suffice.

## Wire Mesh Cages

Heavy-gauge welded wire with openings of 1/2 inch × 1 inch or 1/2 inch × 2 inches can be cut into panels that can be J-clamped together with a special pair of clamping pliers. The clamps and the pliers are sold in feed stores. An all-wire cage is lighter than one of framed of wood, but an all-wire cage lacks some of the structural stability of a wood and wire cage. We have made both fixed (up to 8 ft long, 6 ft high, and 4 ft wide) and movable cages in this manner. The movable cages are simply placed on top of a

When wrapped in heavy pliofilm, outside cages can be used for iguanas even in moderately cool weather.

piece of plywood to which casters have been attached.

Some green iguanas may abrade their noses in cages of this style, especially if the caging does not contain sufficient criss-crosses of limbs and other visual barriers. Keep an eye on any iguanas that you place in these cages to ensure that they are not injuring themselves. If they are, either remove them or renovate the cage.

## The Iguana Room

Some iguanas become so much a part of the family that they are given their own dedicated room. This is an excellent solution to the space problem. It is, of course, mandatory that secured climbing/perching limbs, water receptacles, heating, and lighting are provided.

## Mi Casa Es Su Casa

Many tame iguanas, when their owners are at home, are allowed to roam the entire house, or at least several

A baby iguana may either bask on a sunbathed computer printer or seek cover in a bookcase.

Whether baby or adult, green iguanas often seek the highest possible spot to rest.

rooms. Be certain that all toilets are closed, that all houseplants are non-toxic, that all windows are either closed or have heavy wire over the screens (the claws of a large iguana can inadvertently tear through fiberglass window screens), and that all entryways are tightly closed. Doors on return-springs may injure your iguana. Close the screens on your fireplace, and close the fireplace damper. Lamps that are overturned can cause a fire. Breakable items need to be in an inaccessible room. Remember that salmonella is a normal part of the iguana's bacterial flora. Do not allow your iguana on tables, countertops, or where a baby might crawl.

## Greenhouses

Greenhouses are another housing option, and one many iguana owners choose. These vary from simple, self-standing, fully constructed types available from storage shed dealers to do-it-yourself kits to elaborate house additions that, unless you are very handy, are best left for contractor setup. Greenhouses can be ideal homes for great green iguanas, but absolute security is essential. Additionally, heating and cooling units must be entirely screened to prevent injury to the iguanas. In all cases, double glazing should be considered as an energy-saving option, especially in regions subject to extreme cold or heat.

We further suggest that the base of the unit either be flush against a concrete slab, affixed to a concrete or brick wall, or sunk a foot or more below the surface of the ground. This will preclude any entry by predators and/or escape by the inhabitants.

Greenhouses can bring a few square feet of the tropics to even the

Snowbelt. You can put extensive plantings, climbing limbs, and naturalistic watering, heating, and lighting systems. A small pond and waterfall would not be impossible.

Caution! Watch your dogs when your iguana is loose.

This baby green iguana spends a good deal of time observing us at our computers.

# Cage Furniture for Your Iguana

The great green iguana is one of the more arboreal of lizards. They often bask in the sunlight while sprawled lengthwise along a sturdy limb, drooping their legs and part of their tails over the sides. Always provide your iguana with an elevated basking branch that is at least the diameter of his body, and preferably one and a half times his diameter. The limb(s) must be securely affixed to prevent

When suitably heated, cooled, and ventilated, a greenhouse can be an ideal enclosure for iguanas of any size. Toxic plants should be excluded.

toppling. Direct the warming beams of one (or if your iguana is large, two) floodlight bulbs onto this perch from above. Be certain to position the bulbs so that your iguana will not burn itself if it approaches the lamp. The new-to-the-marketplace, full-spectrum DragonLite seems ideal for this purpose.

We consider "hot rocks" a very unnatural heat source for iguanas. In nature, these lizards warm their bodies from the top down, by orienting and varying their body positions in relation to the warmth provided by and the position of the sun. Warming from the belly up is unnatural, and if your lizard happens to be gravid (pregnant), prolonged basking atop an overwarmed hot rock can cause egg damage.

Providing the security of a hidebox can be of questionable value. Although a hidebox is fine for a completely tame iguana, if the lizard is wild and can conceal itself every time you approach, your iguana may never tame as thoroughly as you would like. Nevertheless, a hidebox does provide a haven for a stressed iguana.

Besides limbs and a hidebox, some keepers prefer to provide their iguana with nontoxic greenery. It is important that, if you use real plants, no insecticides, either contact or systemic, or fertilizers are present. Many persons decorate their iguana enclosures with plastic plants. Iguanas generally test the edibility of these with their tongues and then lose interest.

The floor covering of your cage can consist of any number of items. Newspaper, Kraft paper, Astroturf, indoor/outdoor carpeting, cypress or aspen shavings (cedar can be toxic to your lizard), or even rabbit food (compressed alfalfa pellets) are all ideal. The papers, shavings, and rabbit food can be discarded when soiled; the carpets can be washed when dirty, dried, and replaced.

Many persons have found that their iguanas will repeatedly defecate in a particular area of their cages. Some iguanas choose their water dishes (which must then be cleaned immediately), but others will quickly adopt a kitty pan containing a little sand. The cleaning of the pan is then a simple matter.

# Lighting and Heating

An iguana's position within a cage or in the wild determines how quickly it will warm up in the morning as well as its social position. To elevate its

body temperature as quickly as possible the iguana will seek exposed, sunny limbs and other such promontories where the sun hits first and strong. It will bask until its body temperature has risen to the mid to high 90s. By darkening or lightening its color, and by orienting itself in very specific positions (sideways to the sun when cold or head-on when hot), the iguana can regulate its absorption of heat.

Elevated positions are also used in a king-of-the-mountain manner to display dominance. The most dominant males choose the choicest spot, keeping subordinate males at bay, but sharing the spot with one or more females. In Dade County, Florida, it is no longer unusual to see a huge male iguana, surrounded by 6 to 12 adult females, basking 6 or 8 feet above the ground in a tangle of Brazilian pepper shrub branches. When possible, the big lizards often choose canalside shrubs where they can drop from their

A baby green iguana relaxes fully to bask, but becomes more alert as optimal temperatures are reached.

perch directly into the safety of the water when threatened.

Caged iguanas must be provided with the same opportunity to bask and thermoregulate as the wild specimens. If your iguanas are adult, this requires a large (preferably a room-size) cage. At latitudes south of Tampa Bay in Florida and in Texas' lower Rio Grande Valley, great green iguanas can be kept outdoors for most of the year. In more northerly areas, iguanas can be maintained outdoors during the hottest days of summer but may require cage adaptations if left out over night or on cool days.

It is not difficult to provide lighting for daytime warmth, directed onto a series of limbs. A limb with bark or a chunk of well-weathered, non-pressure-treated fencepost will be much easier for your lizard to climb and cling to than one that has been peeled. If more than one iguana is present, more than one basking station should be provided—each illuminated and warmed. The limb(s) must be securely

affixed, to prevent toppling. Nighttime warmth can be provided by red/blue bulbs, ceramic heating units, or space heaters.

Iguanas are tropical lizards but may occasionally need to cool themselves somewhat. A temperature gradient in the cage is the best way to allow this. The cage temperature should

Sun-warmed blinds are also an easily ascended and fully utilized basking site.

Green iguanas swim readily. This large male, head exposed, is in midpond.

range from 75–80°F on the cool end to 100–105°F on the surface of the basking perch. Make sure your iguana cannot touch any of the heating devices. Iguanas and other reptiles are not capable of realizing that a hot lightbulb will burn them, and many have been severely burned as result.

Until recently we have used large, color-corrected, incandescent plant-growth bulbs in combination with full-spectrum fluorescent bulbs, but we are now experimenting with full-spectrum DragonLite bulbs. DragonLites, designed for incandescent sockets, have only recently appeared on the pet market. There are numerous other incandescent bulbs marketed as "full-spectrum," but read the labeling carefully and choose the bulb that provides ultraviolet rays and is not merely color-corrected.

Outside cages need not be fancy to be effective.

Why bother with ultraviolet (UV) lighting? Is UV lighting actually necessary to the well being of your green iguana? If it is not absolutely necessary, the UV-A and UV-B rays they produce are unquestionably beneficial. UV-A helps promote natural behavior in reptiles (see cautions in handling, page 24), and UV-B, controls the synthesis of vitamin $D_3$ in the reptile's skin. When natural synthesis occurs, it allows greater error in feeding supplements.

Although the true benefits to your lizard from artificial sources is conjectural, the benefit from one lighting source is not—and this source is as close as your back door.

Natural, unfiltered sunlight unquestionably provides the best possible lighting (and heat) for iguanas. You may have been wondering why we suggested that your cages always be able to pass through your doorways and be on casters. Here is why: it will allow you to move your lizards—still securely caged—outdoors on warm, sunny days. In most cases the casters will allow a single person to accomplish this otherwise unwieldy task. There is simply nothing better that you can do for your lizards.

**Caution:** Only cages constructed of wood and wire should be placed out in the sun, and even those should be watched closely until the temperatures attained within are truly determined. A glass terrarium not only filters out the UV but also concentrates and holds the sun's heat, even with a screen top or no top. This can literally cook your iguanas in just a few minutes' time, even on a relatively cool day! Be sure to provide a shaded area for your lizard even in the wood and wire cages.

If you live in an area where it is absolutely impossible to get your lizard outside, perhaps you could allow it to bask in a screened, opened window on hot summer days. Natural, unfiltered sunlight from any vantage point will be of benefit.

To make this possible for more hobbyists, a "window cage" that slides in and out of an opened window on extendable tracks has been developed. This should prove to be a real boon to apartment, condo, or city dwellers who would be otherwise unable to allow their young iguana access to natural sunlight.

Rather than a purchase of a window cage, you may choose to just use a cage of wood and wire or of wire panels J-clamped together. This can be hooked or wedged into a window, and although less convenient than a cage on tracks, it will suffice.

Remember the earlier admonitions regarding excessive heat buildup. Monitor the temperatures in the cage carefully at all times and provide a shaded area to which your iguana can retreat if it chooses.

# Altering Humidity

Proper cage humidity is an important, but often overlooked aspect of herpetoculture. Your iguana is adapted to high humidity situations and may experience shedding and other problems if cage humidity is too low. Cage humidity can be increased by using a larger water dish, misting the cage interior, or decreasing the amount of ventilation.

If you have a "house iguana," all foliage plants must be nontoxic.

# Feeding Your Iguana

## Understanding Diets

The dietary needs of iguanas in general and of the great green iguana in particular have been the subject of years of study by field observers and by reptile nutritionists. Today, although we categorize the great green iguana as a primarily (or wholly) folivorous species, there is less harmony beyond that point.

Because animal protein is known to cause visceral gout and other health problems in captive iguanas, the current train of thought is that these lizards do not voluntarily eat animal protein in the wild. This seems to depend on geographic area and the

Dark leafy greens are among the best dietary items for green iguanas.

iguana population. I (RDB) have sat in iguana habitats in several Latin American countries and watched wild baby iguanas animatedly chase down and eat many species of insects. I have seen the same behavior exhibited by feral iguanas in Dade County, Florida.

What isn't known is whether these wild and feral iguanas that eat animal protein develop the same health problems as captive iguanas fed animal protein. It could be that with normal exercise, natural sunlight, and the foliage diet, the seemingly deleterious effects of animal protein in the diet of wild iguanas is lessened or nullified.

Captive green iguanas fed even moderate amounts of animal protein often develop gout and bone problems. We do not yet know whether captive iguanas kept outside are less prone to these problems than green iguanas kept inside.

Until much more is known with certainty about the diet of a green iguana and its effects under all circumstances, you should feed your iguana vegetables. Err on the side of caution if you are to err at all. We further feel that a large cage in which your iguana may exercise and full-spectrum lighting (or, better yet, natural, unfiltered sunlight) will help offset any mistakes you might make.

Vitamin and mineral additives will help offset any dietary deficiencies.

Iguanas—all reptiles, in fact—are very slow to show the results of an improper diet. Months, or even more than a year, may pass before external signs are manifested. In most cases, an improper diet is signified by metabolic bone disease, or MBD. Captive iguanas with chubby hind legs and shortened noses display this malady. What has happened is that calcium has been leached from the bones to maintain calcium levels in the blood. Sadly, once the external manifestations are apparent, it is often either impossible or at least very difficult to reverse the progression of the problem(s). Certainly, the best approach is prevention.

We consider dietary items such as insects, pinky mice, moistened or rehydrated dog or cat foods, monkey chow, or other such materials improper for captive green iguanas in amounts any greater than a *very* occasional treat.

The diet that you are striving to provide is one in which the ratio of calcium to phosphorus is 2 or 3 to 1. Provide your pet iguana with a varied diet, all the while remembering that, as far as food values go, not even all

A dealer's holding cage for newly imported baby iguanas.

Windowsill gardens are favorite snacking for baby green iguanas.

vegetables are created equal. Some vegetables, such as iceberg (sandwich) lettuce, have an unsatisfactory ratio of phosphorus to calcium. Spinach contains oxalic acid, a calcium binder. These vegetables are not a satisfactory food for an iguana.

When using leafy vegetables, choose those that are the darkest. Romaine, escarole, turnip greens, collards, mustard greens, dandelion greens and flowers, bok choy, and nasturtiums (all parts) are all excellent foods. Rose and hibiscus blossoms are also appreciated, as are unsweetened bran cereals, alfalfa pellets and sprouts, clover leaves and blossoms, beans (including leaves and stems), grated squash, apples, various hays and grasses, and grain breads. Tofu and other soybean products are fine foods and are often enjoyed by iguanas. A greater variety of foods will usually be accepted by your iguana if the veggies are chopped into small pieces and mixed together. Place the food in a dish so that your iguana can eat readily without ingesting any substrate.

## Vitamin-Mineral Supplements

Calcium/$D_3$ supplements are beneficial to iguanas, especially those that do not have access to natural, unfiltered sunlight. Powdered calcium alone may not be properly metabolized. Fast-growing baby iguanas and ovulating females will need frequent supplementation; half grown to fully grown males will need the least. For ovulating females and baby iguanas, we suggest multivitamin/calcium/$D_3$

supplementation every second day. The diet of fully grown male lizards may be supplemented once weekly. We have used Osteoform for many years and have not observed any unwanted side effects.

## Correcting Your Iguana's Diet

There are times when you may acquire an iguana that has long been maintained on an incorrect diet. Because it may take months or even years for the effects of an improper diet to be reflected in declining health, your new lizard may appear entirely normal in all respects. However, be assured that if over time the diet remains incorrect, your animal's health will eventually be seriously compromised. The diet must be corrected.

In the ideal case scenario, your iguana would just begin eating the new diet when you presented it. However, that is seldom the case, especially if the iguana has eaten a specific item over a long period. Then, it may be necessary to resort to gentle subterfuge to effect the necessary diet change. Begin, of course, by mixing the new dietary components with the old. It may be necessary to dice all finely and mix them thoroughly, but sometimes this works. If your iguana refuses the new diet, don't worry—yet. Present it daily. If your iguana continues to pick out only its favored items, a finer puree may make this selection impossible. Iguanas will also be more apt to accept a change in diet if they are hungry. To add this increment to a food change, merely withhold all food for a day or two, keeping in mind the size and condition of your lizard. Continue to provide water for your iguana in the normal fashion during this changeover. You want it to be hungry, not dehydrated.

## Toxic Plants

Many lists of so-called toxic plants have been compiled, but keep in mind that what is toxic to humans may not be toxic to animals. Poison ivy berries and mushrooms known to be poisonous to humans are eaten with impunity by many creatures. So are many of the more toxic fruits of solanaceous plants (nightshades). What is fatally poisonous to one group of animals may be a delicacy to others. In the wild, reptiles probably recognize naturally occurring potentially problematic plants by odor or by the merest taste.

Many lily-relative plants, such as this climbing onion, contain toxins that may be fatal if your iguana eats them.

## Suggested Food Plants

Listed here are some plants that are known to be safe foods for your iguana. Besides these plants, there are many other safe and nutritious plants. Please remember that the listing does not include food value. It merely means that this plant is a nontoxic (safe) food for your iguana (or other herbivorous reptile).

Alfalfa
Apple
Avocado
Berries (strawberries, blueberries, elderberries, etc.)
Bok choy
Bread
Broccoli stems and leaves
Cabbage
Dandelions
Escarole
Grated root crops (carrots, beets, etc.)
Grated squashes
Greens (collard, mustard, beet)
Hibiscus blooms and leaves
Kale
Leaf lettuces (dark types)
Melons
Nasturtium
Okra
Papaya
Peaches
Pear
Plums
Romaine
Rose petals
Tofu
Tomato

**Note:** Iguanas should not eat vegetables that contain a high percentage of available phosphorus and/or oxalic acid. The diet of an iguana, or any other herbivorous lizard should provide a much higher percentage of calcium than phosphorus, and should include few, if any, plants that would inhibit calcium metabolization. Typical examples of calcium binders are spinach and wood sorrel. The minimum ratio of calcium to phosphorus would be 2:1; a slightly higher level of calcium would be better. To find out the calcium:phosphorous content of a food plant, consult publications such as the *Composition of Foods*, Handbook Number 8, published by the USDA in 1983.

Many types of commercially prepared iguana diets are now available. Most are advertised as being a "complete diet." Some have been subjected to veterinary scrutiny for their overall suitability and found to be wanting. One was found to be quite unpalatable. Others seem quite satisfactory. Although it is not our intent to promote or decry the effectiveness of any prepared food, we do not advocate the use of any one as a complete diet. Rather, we suggest that if you do choose to use a prepared iguana diet, that you augment it with fresh vegetables. Under normal conditions, iguanas metabolize a fair percentage of their moisture requirements from their fresh vegetable diet. Prepared iguana diets are often pelleted and drier than fresh foliage; thus they provide little moisture to your iguana and can contribute to dehydration and constipation. To help offset a potential problem, you may wish to presoak the pellets in clean water. In any case, when feeding an iguana a commercially prepared iguana diet, always have a supply of clean, fresh water readily accessible.

# Water

In the wild, the great green iguana is a multielement lizard. It climbs trees admirably, runs swiftly over bare ground and through dauntingly tangled underbrush, and readily drops from well-elevated perches into forest streams and rivers and swims rapidly away.

Water, both for drinking and for bathing, as well as for proper hydration, is of extreme importance to your iguana. Because iguanas often defecate in standing water, their receptacle should be cleaned and sterilized as needed, at least once every 3 days. Not to do so may promote bacterial or protozoan growth resulting in adverse health implications.

Mike Beaver's young male iguana was a veritable chowhound. It fed readily even while being held.

# Health

## General Maintenance Notes

Although they are not necessarily compelling health concerns, certain facets of your iguana's life may need occasional addressing.

### Nail Trimming

An iguana's claws grow throughout the lizard's life. As would be expected from a lizard with arboreal propensities, the curved claws are heavy and

Curious or frightened iguanas easily suspend themselves by one foot.

tipped with a sharp sheath that allows not only an easy ascent but a certain degree of agility in the trees as well. In nature, the tip of the claw is usually kept worn well down. Because of the reduced activity available to most captive iguanas, the claws often grow inordinately long and must be trimmed periodically.

Restraining an iguana to trim its claws can be traumatic for even a tame lizard and might well result in your being bitten during the process.

An iguana's claws are sensitive and contain a central vein that runs nearly to the tip. It is important that this vein, often referred to as the quick, not be severed during the trimming process. To ascertain this, only the very tip—the narrow sharp point—of each claw should be removed. Bleeding will occur—and your iguana will try desperately to escape your grasp or may bite—if you cut too high. If this happens, the blood flow should be staunched by applying a styptic powder.

Wrapping the iguana in a soft towel and covering its head to prevent sudden movement and to reduce the possibility of being bitten is an acceptable and suggested approach.

Reptile-oriented veterinarians will cut your iguana's claws if you choose not to.

## Skin Shedding

Reptiles, including iguanas, periodically shed their skin. In snakes, the skin is usually shed in a single piece. Some lizards also shed theirs in a single piece, but usually not as neatly as a snake. However, most lizards, again including iguanas, normally shed their skin in patchwork fashion over a period of days. Provided your iguana is adequately hydrated and its cage humidity is sufficiently high, shedding will pose no problems. You may see your iguana scratching itself or rubbing against perches, or even walls of its cage, to free itself from loosening patches of skin. It is particularly important that all skin is shed from the toes and tail, lest it dry into a constricting band, impair circulation, and result in the loss of that toe or tailtip. A shed that remains on a dorsal spine may eventually result in the loss of that spine. By the same token, if a piece of shedding skin is removed before the new skin beneath is fully ready, scarring and other problems may result.

Misting or bathing your iguana may help facilitate the manual removal of a piece of skin. For a particularly difficult shed, dab on a tiny bit of mineral oil and massage it in, and then gently manually remove the patch. A solution is now available in most pet stores that, if applied to a piece of sticking skin, will also soften and help remove it.

Be assiduous but not overzealous about skin removal.

## Sneezing

Although sneezing is often associated with respiratory distress, more often than not a sneeze is your iguana's way of ridding itself of salt accumulations in the nasal passages and around the nostrils. This is entirely normal and is not cause for concern.

## Broken Tails

Although iguanas do not autotomize (break off) their tail as readily as some lizards, their tail will break under duress. It will not regenerate as fully as the tail of some other lizards. Because the fracture planes (actual breaking points within the tail vertebrae) are better defined when the lizards are young, baby iguanas both break and regenerate their tails more readily than older specimens. A break near the tip will regenerate more fully than a proximal break (an incomplete break may occasionally result in the formation of a second tail). With growth, the fracture planes fuse, and regeneration becomes cursory.

Autotomy is a natural phenomenon normally accompanied by little bleeding and seldom requires veterinary attention. It is, of course, best to avoid a broken tail if possible. Usually the loss of a tail is the result of the tail being grasped by the owner or by a family pet. Never—repeat never—lift, grasp, or restrain your iguana by its tail.

A portrait of a normal baby green iguana.

## Broken Limbs, Toes, and Claws

Iguanas are designed by Mother Nature to be able to drop long distances without injury. A drop from an elevated perch into a river or onto a leafy substrate is less dangerous than a drop onto cement or another hard surface. Yet, if your iguana is in good condition, even this latter drop may not result in injury. However, if dietary calcium is insufficient, or the metabolism of calcium is impaired, even a short drop, an abrupt stop, or the restraint of an excited iguana by a limb can result in a break. Any broken limb should be assessed immediately by a qualified reptile veterinarian.

Toes break more easily than limbs, but the injury is less serious. A claw snagged in caging wire or a narrow crack in cage furniture or elsewhere can result in a break. Many vet-erinarians will amputate, rather than set a badly broken toe. After the expected initial discomfort, your iguana will climb, walk, and run as efficiently with 19 toes as with 20.

Instead of a toe break, the snagging of a claw by your iguana may result in the claw being broken or actually pulled out. This can be accompanied by considerable bleeding, which may require both direct pressure and styptic to staunch. If any core material is left, the claw will often fully regrow.

# Diseases

### Metabolic Bone Disease

The technical names for metabolic bone disease (MBD) are nutritional secondary hyperthyroidism and fibrous osteodystrophy. In simplified terms, MBD is the utilization of bone calcium deposits by the iguana to sustain life. It is manifested by, among other symptoms, softened and foreshortened jawbones and swollen, pliable limbs due to demineralized bones.

MBD has been the subject of many discussions and articles, some on a technical and others on a layman's level. This insidious problem, found among herbivorous lizards, is also referred to in some of its forms as rickets and demineralization. It is firmly associated with an improper diet.

The cause of MBD is a lack of calcium; the result is an improper ratio of phosphorus to the available calcium. A lack of vitamin $D_3$ and a diet heavy in calcium binders, which remove available calcium, will contribute to the problem. You need to monitor the calcium:phosphorus of

Baby green iguanas may warm themselves atop lampshades.

the diet and dietary additives, so as to keep the intake of calcium not only sufficient but also twice that of phosphorus. This is simple, once you know what foods to offer (and what not to offer—see the chapter on diet).

Unless your iguana has access to unfiltered sunlight, you'll need also to provide a vitamin $D_3$ source. Your iguana needs vitamin $D_3$ to metabolize calcium. Natural sunlight induces normal $D_3$ synthesis, which, in turn, permits the metabolism of calcium.

How do all these problems affect the iguana? To exist, all creatures need a certain level of blood calcium. When the level of blood calcium drops below a certain percentage, the parathyroid glands begin the complex process of drawing calcium from the bones to the blood. As the bones lose their rigidity, parts of them become overlaid with a fibrous tissue in an effort to compensate for the loss of bone strength. Deformities occur, and the bones are easily broken.

Although MBD is treatable, it is not often completely reversible. A good iguana diet that is rich in calcium, with vitamin $D_3$ additives, will begin the treatment process. If the iguana already displays the characteristic chubby hind legs and a pug-nosed look to its face, veterinary assessment and intervention is mandatory. That treatment will probably begin with an injection of liquid calcium and will include further medications and supplements to the corrected diet.

## Respiratory Ailments

Unless they are debilitated, iguanas are not particularly prone to respiratory ailments. Debilitation can be caused by, among other conditions, perpetual stress (including stress caused by untenable loads of endoparasites), marginal health, and improper temperatures.

Respiratory ailments are indicated by sneezing, lethargic demeanor, and unnaturally rapid, often shallow, breathing. As the disease progresses, rasping and bubbling may accompany each of your lizard's breaths. At this stage, the respiratory ailment is often critical and can be fatal.

Begin by separating the lizard from any cage mates and then elevating the temperature in its basking area (*not* the entire cage) to about 100°F. The more optimal its surroundings, the better able the specimen is to deal with a respiratory ailment. Food should be available, although the iguana may not feed for a while.

The rest of the cage should be retained at its usual temperature. If the symptoms of respiratory ailment distress do not greatly lessen within a day or two, do not delay any longer. Call your veterinarian, and take your iguana to him or her for antibiotic treatment.

There are many "safe" drugs available, but some respiratory ailments do not respond well to these. The newer aminoglycoside drugs and others, newer still, are more effective, but they are correspondingly more dangerous. There is little latitude in dosage amounts, and the lizard must be well hydrated to ensure against renal (kidney) damage. The injection site for aminoglycosides should be anterior to midbody to avoid damaging the kidneys.

## Endoparasites

The presence of internal parasites in lizards from the wild is a foregone conclusion. However, fewer hobbyists realize that captive-bred and hatched lizards may also harbor endoparasites. Roundworms, pinworms, nematodes, tapeworms, and/or parasitic protozoans may all be found. We feel that whether or not the lizard is treated for endoparasites depends on the health of each individual lizard, as demonstrated by its behavior.

Certainly the problems created by endoparasitic loads in weakened lizards need be addressed promptly. However, if the specimen in question is bright-eyed, alert, and feeding well and has a good color, you may wish to forego an immediate veterinary treatment. Endoparasitic loads can actually diminish if you keep the cage of your specimen scrupulously clean, thereby preventing reinfestation.

Getting rid of endoparasites means administering a substance that is toxic to the parasites in dosages that will not harm the lizard. Obviously, dosages must be accurate, which is why you need your veterinarian's assistance. It is very easy for a layperson to miscalculate metric conversions or to fail to actually get the correct dosage into the lizard. The result may be fatal or futile. Let your reptile veterinarian do the work for which he or she was trained.

## Ectoparasites

External parasites are less problematic to treat than endoparasites. Only ticks are seen with any regularity on iguanas. Ticks are flattened and seedlike in appearance when empty, rounded and bladderlike when engorged. It is best if they are removed whenever seen. They embed their mouthparts deeply when feeding, and if merely pulled from the lizard these may break off in the wound. It is best to dust them individually with Sevin powder first and then to return a few

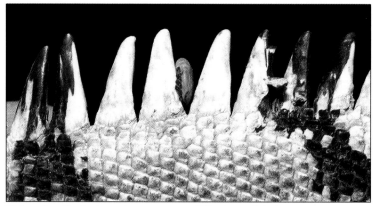

Ticks often feed where they are most difficult to dislodge, as between the crest scales of this spiny-tailed iguana.

minutes later and pull the ticks gently off with a pair of tweezers. A tick-removing implement is now available; this consists of a spring-loaded pair of tweezers in a cylindrical tube. After grasping the tick, you rotate the implement, an action that safely removes the entire tick.

## Other Maladies

Several other diseases and maladies may rarely occur. Among these are:

- Mineralization of internal organs: This is caused by the overmetabolizing of calcium, or overdosing with $D_3$. Known as hypercalcemia, a treatment has now been developed but is both lengthy and expensive. Treatment requires about 2 weeks of monitoring by a veterinarian. There is a fine line between too much and not enough calcium and vitamin $D_3$. Once it is diagnosed and corrected, you'll need to reduce both calcium and $D_3$ intake by your specimen. If untreated or too far advanced, this can become a fatal problem. Do remember that an iguana with access to natural, unfiltered sunlight will require less calcium–$D_3$ dietary additive than an iguana having no access to sunlight.
- Hypoglycemia: This relates to low blood sugar. Stress or pancreatic dysfunction can be the causative agent. The stress factor is correctable; the problem with the pancreas, most commonly caused by an insulin-secreting tumor, usually is not.

## Medical Treatments for Internal Parasites

Because of the complexities of identification of endoparasites and the necessity to weigh your iguana accurately, the eradication of internal parasites is best left to a qualified reptile veterinarian. So that you'll know what some of the treatments are and can discuss them with your veterinarian, here are a few of the recommended medications and dosages.

### Amoebas and Trichomonads

For amoebas and trichomonads, one treatment of 40–50 mg/kg of metronidazole is given orally. The treatment is repeated in 2 weeks. Dimetridazole can also be used, but the dosage is very different. For 5 days, 40–50 mg/kg of dimetrizadole is administered daily. The treatment is then repeated in 2 weeks. All treatments with both medications are administered once daily.

### Coccidia

Many treatments are available. The dosages of sulfadiazine, sulfamerazine, and sulfamethazine are identical. Administer 75 mg/kg the first day; then follow up for the next 5 days with 45 mg/kg. All treatments are administered orally and repeated once daily. Sulfadimethoxine is also effective. The initial dosage is 90 mg/kg orally to be followed for the next 5 days with 45 mg/kg orally. All dosages are administered once daily. Trimethoprim-sulfa may also be used by administering 30 mg/kg once daily for 7 days.

### Cestodes (Tapeworms)

Several effective treatments are available. Bunamidine may be administered orally at a dosage of 50 mg/kg. A second treatment occurs in 14 days. Niclosamide, given orally at a dosage of 150 mg/kg, is also effective. A second treatment is given in 2 weeks. Finally, praziquantel may be administered either orally or intramuscularly. The dosage is 5–8 mg/kg and is to be repeated in 14 days.

### Trematodes (Flukes)
Praziquantel at 8 mg/kg may be administered either orally or intramuscularly. The treatment is repeated in 2 weeks.

### Nematodes (Roundworms)
Several effective treatments are available. Levamisol, an injectable intraperitoneal treatment, should be administered at a dosage of 10 mg/kg, and the treatment should be repeated in 2 weeks. Ivermectin, injected intramuscularly in a dosage of 200 (µg/kg is effective. The treatment is to be repeated in 2 weeks. Ivermectin can be toxic to certain taxa (ball pythons are one example) but not to iguanas. Thiabendazole and fenbendazole have similar dosages. Both are administered orally at 50–100 mg/kg and repeated in 14 days. Mebendazole is administered orally at a dosage of 20–25 mg/kg and is repeated in 14 days.

Baby green iguanas learn computer skills early in life.

# Breeding

## Courtship and Reproduction

The great green iguana is an oviparous lizard. Wild females in a given population ovulate at pretty much the same time every year, but in captivity, this may not be true. In captivity, the day length and the ambient temperatures can be controlled, both of which affect breeding readiness. Captive iguanas have bred in October, some as late as June, and others in the months between. It is not unlikely that we soon will have records for captive iguana breeding during all months of the year.

This impressive male green iguana is from a non-orange population.

Some adult male green iguanas become suffused with orange during the breeding season.

Male green iguanas herald reproductive readiness with enhanced color, increased alertness, territorial and courtship displays, and less tolerance (and sometimes aggression) for normal overtures by their keeper. Females may become slightly more fussy as feeders and less willing to be handled by their owners, but overall their breeding readiness response is less obvious than the males.

The breeding colors of the males vary by geographic origin of the lizard, from a brilliant green to any one of several shades of orange. Some males may display vertical black bars on their sides. Courtship behaviors include rapid distending and furling of the dewlap, rapid head-bobs, a side-to-side flattening of the body (this makes the iguana look larger), full extension of the forelimbs, and anterior push-ups. When this behavior is noted, be very careful when approaching a dominant male.

In a study made of green iguanas in Costa Rica, R. Wayne Van Devender found that females may move to the territory of a large potential mate, or the male may seek out and move onto the tree of a likely looking female. It is not unusual for a female in a tree to be courted by two males at the same time, with the female moving to the tree of the male she selects. A single male may court and win two receptive females within his territory. Paired iguanas stay together for a minimum of 4 weeks before copulation actually occurs. Courtship display bouts occur between the pairs prior to breeding, with the duration of the displays shortening with successive breedings.

The receptive female iguana may approach or ignore a displaying male. She may show her readiness to be bred by her own set of head-bobs and forebody push-ups. The male will approach, grasp her by the side of her neck in his jaws, twist his tail under hers, and insert one of his hemipenes.

In Miami, Florida, a patch of orange atop a fence may well be an adult male green iguana in breeding color.

When we got close, we saw that this huge male iguana (center) was accompanied by more than eight adult females.

If successful, copulation lasts from a few minutes to about a quarter of an hour. Breeding may be repeated up to five times between the pair before the female's receptiveness ends. If a male has more than one female in his harem, he will court each one daily but may mate with them on alternate days.

If you keep your iguanas together all the time, you may or may not witness the breeding. If you separate your iguanas just before breeding season, but re-introduce them to each other for supervised periods, you will probably see the breeding take place. If the iguanas are kept where they can see each other as a matter of course, most of the courtship process can take place whether you're home or not. The re-introduction should certainly have its desired effect.

As might be expected, after being grasped by a male, the neck of a female iguana may become from moderately to seriously abraded. Males will attempt to breed so persistently that it may be necessary to separate the pair to prevent serious injury to the female. It is best if there is not a significant difference in size between the two.

In the wild, smaller males that have not won females of their own do not give up easily. A smaller male may use subterfuge, approaching the female from above and from behind leafy branches when the dominant male is not paying attention. The smaller male will leap onto the back of the female and attempt to mate. The female will abruptly decline, with gaped mouth and violent twisting of the body, the attentions of the smaller male. If the dominant male notices, he will head-butt the interloper out of the tree.

# Conditioning and Breeding Great Green Iguanas

There are two distinctly different levels of breeding green iguanas in captivity: large-scale farming and small- scale breeding programs.

Farming these magnificent lizards is a rather new concept and is now practiced widely in many Latin American countries. From dozens to hundreds of breeder iguanas are housed and allowed to breed in outdoor pens. Hatchlings produced at these farming operations are being used both in an attempt to enhance dwindling wild populations (due to habitat destruction and past collection for the pet market) and as a cash-crop for the pet trade. This latter has resulted in hatchling iguanas being readily and inexpensively available during much of the year.

Hobbyists also breed iguanas, but only in small numbers. Because the lizards are so inexpensive, they breed them usually as a labor of love, not for their commercial value. Although green iguanas often breed well in captivity, there are some guidelines, other than the spacious facilities dictated by their large adult size, that will help ascertain your success.

## Cycling

Naturally occurring seasonal climatic changes such as photoperiod, temperature, rainfall, and relative humidity influence the life cycle of the iguana. These changes are no less important in captivity than in the wild. If you are among the growing number of iguana owners who live in the Sunbelt, and especially in southern Florida and the lower Rio Grande Valley of Texas, and if you keep your iguana outside whenever possible, Mother Nature will oversee some, if not most, of these necessary changes.

However, if you maintain your iguana indoors, it is likely that you will need to provide Mother Nature an assist. In captivity, certain of these cyclic stimuli can and should be approximated when preparing your iguanas for breeding. Others can be ignored.

The term *photoperiod* simply refers to the hours of daylight (as opposed to the hours of darkness) in any given day. Photoperiod is more seasonally variable at (or near) the poles than at the equator. The hours of daylight increase as winter gives way to spring and spring to summer and then decrease again in the autumn. We suggest that a natural photoperiod is best. Check the weather page in your local newspaper for the exact sunrise and sunset times and periodically (about weekly) alter the number of hours that your cage is artificially illuminated to coincide with the naturally occurring photoperiod. If you happen to be keeping your lizard in outside caging, allow the photoperiod to be natural. Your iguana will be active only during the hours of daylight. When necessary, photoperiod can be altered with the use of brilliant lighting, but, generally speaking, you should provide the lowest humidity, the fewest hours of daylight, and the lowest temperatures in midwinter.

Temperatures, both daily and seasonal, can be altered with the prudent use of lights and/or heating elements. Iguanas are subjected in the wild to one or two rapid drops of several degrees in temperature daily brought about by rainstorms. It is not necessary to duplicate these minifluctuations of temperature to facilitate breeding. There is a winter drop in relative humidity (likely in captivity as well) during that season, and a several degree drop of nighttime temperature. If you are trying to elevate nighttime temperatures, use a ceramic heater or a red or a blue bulb. It would seem that the light from either is less intrusive than from a white bulb.

To produce healthy eggs that develop into robust hatchlings, your breeder iguanas must themselves be in good condition. They should have good body weight, be free of excessive burdens of endoparasites, have had ample full-spectrum lighting, and be fully hydrated. Do not breed them otherwise. Relative humidity should always be high within the cage and can be increased, if necessary, by providing a larger water bowl, by misting the cage daily, or by altering air flow through the cage. A completely or partially covered cage containing a sizable water dish will be more humid than a well-ventilated terrarium containing a small water bowl.

Your lizards should be fed heavily throughout the year. Because appetites wane for 2 to 4 weeks prior to egg deposition, it is particularly important that your iguanas enter the breeding period in A-1 condition. Be sure to provide sufficient calcium and $D_3$ throughout the year. These additives are especially important when the females are laying down eggshells. If your female becomes dehydrated while she is carrying eggs, it may be difficult for her to lay.

# Nests and Nesting

During the periods of reduced light, temperature, humidity, and rainfall, reduction by the iguana in the production of certain key hormones cause ovarian and testicular regression. With the lengthening days and correspondingly increasing warmth, humidity, and rain activity of spring and summer, hormonal production again increases, causing the changes that stimulate interest in reproduction. With the increase in the production of testosterone also come increased interest in territoriality with a correspondingly increased aggressive attitude toward rival males. It is at this time that what may have until then been compatible groups of iguanas are apt to become quarrelsome.

Female iguanas put their all into nesting preparations. After choosing a suitable site, she will use her forefeet to dig deeply into the earth. Loosened dirt and debris is removed with the rear feet. When finished, the hole will be sufficiently large for the female to seclude herself completely while laying and may have one or more side chambers. Usually, several times during preparations, the female will back into the egg site to peer quizzically from the deepening depression, perhaps scouting for approaching danger. Certainly while digging, she is more vulnerable to predation than at almost any other time in her life.

The nesting efforts may be curtailed at any time during the preparation. If disturbed by a predator or if the digging is thwarted by a maze of roots or rocks, the female will often leave to begin anew elsewhere at another time. Even if completed after several periods of digging interspersed with periods of rest, the female, based upon criteria known best to her, may deem the nesting chamber unsuitable. Should this be the case, she'll abandon the completed but unused nest and proceed anew at another location and another time. If the female is unable to find and complete a satisfactory nest, she may become egg-bound, and veterinary intervention will be needed. Symptoms include a bloated appearance, restlessness, and failure to feed. Even unmated females can produce eggs and become egg-bound.

However, if all is deemed well with the initial excavation, the female will, after a period of rest, lay and position each egg of her clutch. Then she will fill the hole with the removed dirt and leave. Dependent on temperature and moisture, the period of incubation can and will vary considerably. At the low end, under ideal nest conditions, the eggs may hatch in about 70 days. Under cooler, dryer conditions, the incubation may near a full 3 months.

Tame, calm, and healthy iguanas make the best breeders. If your iguanas are fearful and skittish, breeding sequences are easily interrupted. You can lessen the chances of problems by allowing your female to become accustomed to the nesting chamber prior to egg deposition and by having your incubator set and ready.

Iguanas kept out-of-doors in the southernmost areas of our country can be allowed to breed and nest nearly like they would in the wild. We, as owners, merely need to ascertain that suitable nesting areas are present in the cages. In some of the more ideally arranged cages, the female iguana will construct her own nest in much the way she would in the wild. If she does not initially begin her own nest (and you feel the substrate is suitable), merely disturbing the surface of the ground may be an adequate prompt. Occasionally a female can be induced to nest naturally by providing her with a secluded area (such as the bottom third of a *large*, dark-colored plastic trash can with an entryhole cut in it, inverted over the most suitable spot) within which she may dig. In other cases, where caging conditions are less natural, a suitable nesting chamber must be constructed for the female iguana.

Several nest models seem equally well accepted by gravid female iguanas. Suitability seems governed by four considerations, these being adequate amounts of space and darkness as well as appropriate moisture content and temperature.

An in-ground nest can easily be made in one of two ways: by digging down and framing an adequately sized depression with wood or by sinking the inverted bottom third of a large, dark-colored (dark brown or black), heavy plastic trash can in the ground. In either case, an entryway must be left open. You will need to cover the wooden chamber with a piece of plywood or other suitably opaque top. The gravid female iguana may either deposit her eggs right in this chamber as provided or scratch an additional depression in the dirt that the chamber covers. Although many breeders feel that iguanas favor rather long entranceways to their in-ground nesting chambers, the long entranceways are certainly not mandatory. However, should you decide to provide one, it is easily made by burying one or more lengths of ceramic pipe of suitable diameter (end to end if more than a single piece is

used), sloping them from the surface to the entrance of the main nesting chamber.

An above-ground nest can be easily made by utilizing a large, dark-colored, rigid plastic trash can. A can with four flat sides is the easiest to work with. Choose an area of the pen where the can will not overheat. Cut an entrance hole in an upper corner of the top. Securely affix the top to the bottom. Lay the can on one of its broad sides. Half fill the entire length of the horizontal can with a barely moistened mixture of half sand/half soil. A little peat can be mixed in to help retain moisture and lighten the mixture somewhat. This trash can arrangement may also be used successfully in indoor settings.

## Eggs and Incubation

Green iguanas may lay from 10 to 70 (rarely more) eggs. An average clutch from a healthy adult female numbers between 35 and 45 eggs. The eggs are laid about 70–85 days following copulation. The eggs have a pliable (and permeable) parchmentlike shell.

A green iguana hatches from an egg incubated on a substrate of moistened perlite.

Their permeable eggshells allow the eggs to desiccate or overhydrate quite easily. Watch the eggs closely during incubation. If the eggs begin to collapse, increase the moisture *slightly*; if they get turgid and slick, decrease the moisture. Do note, however, that even under ideal incubation conditions, when full term is neared, dimpling and a concurrent lack of eggshell turgidity is normal.

At a temperature of 85–87°F, incubation takes from 60 to nearly 80 days.

## Incubation

Following deposition, remove the eggs as soon as possible for incubation. It seems best, but may not be as critical as we once thought, if the orientation in which the egg was found is not changed. (In other words, just to be safe, keep the same side up.)

The chosen incubation medium (perlite, vermiculite, or sphagnum moss) should be moistened. Start with equal parts of water and medium by weight, and add water until the medium clumps when squeezed in your hand, but you cannot wring any water out of it. The end result should be that the medium is moist but not wet. Place 1–1.5 inches of the medium in the bottom of a nonventilated plastic shoe box. The eggs of iguanas should be at least one-half to two-thirds buried in the substrate. Once the eggs are in place, put the lid on the shoe box(es) and place it (them) in the incubator. A shallow open dish of water in the incubator will help keep the relative humidity high. You may need to add water to the medium (not onto the eggs) to keep the moisture level.

Although the sex of many lizard species is determined by the temperature at which the egg was incubated (temperature-dependent sex determination), this does not seem to be so with iguanas. Both males and females are produced at all suitable incubation temperatures (genetically determined sex).

### Making Your Own Incubator

Materials needed for one incubator include:

1 wafer thermostat/heater (obtainable from feed stores; these are commonly used in incubators for chicks)

1 thermometer

1 Styrofoam cooler—one with thick sides (a fish-shipping box is ideal)

1 heat tape

3 wire nuts

piece of heavy wire mesh, bent in a U-shape to use as a shelf for the egg container

Make a hole through the lid of the Styrofoam cooler, and suspend the thermostat/heater from the inside. The wiring for the thermostat/heater should be on the inside of the lid. Add another hole for a thermometer so that you can check on the inside temperature without opening the top. (If there's no flange on the thermometer to keep it from slipping through the hole in the lid, use a rubber band wound several times around the thermometer to form a flange.)

Your goal is to wire the thermostat between the heat tape and the electrical cord, in order to regulate the amount of heat produced by the heat tape.

Cut the electrical cord off the heat tape, leaving about 18 inches of the cord on the heat tape. Make a hole through the side of the Styrofoam box, about 5 inches below the top edge. Pull the electrical cord through the hole, leaving the plug end outside (don't plug it in just yet!). Strip off about a half-inch of the insulation from the wiring at the cut end, and separate the two wires for a few inches.

Coil the heat tape loosely in the bottom of the Styrofoam box, making sure that it doesn't cross over itself at any point. Coil the tape so the recently cut end is near the electrical cord. Strip off about a half-inch of the insulation from the end of the wiring, and separate the two wires for a few inches.

Using one of the wire nuts, connect one of the red wires of the thermostat to one of the electrical wires of the heat tape. Use a second nut to connect the second red wire of the thermostat to one of the wires of the electrical cord. The third nut is used to connect the second wire of the electrical cord to the second wire of the heat tape (in effect, reestablishing part of the original wiring between the heat tape and its electrical cord.)

That's all there is to it. Put the lid on the cooler, and plug in the thermostat/heater. Wait half an hour and check the temperature. The L-shaped pin on the top of the thermostat is the rheostat; turn it to increase or decrease the temperature inside your new incubator. You want the inside to be 80–86°F (27–30°C).

Once you have the temperature regulated, add your hardware cloth "shelf," and put the container of eggs atop the shelf. Close the egg container.

Check the temperature daily and add a little water to the incubating medium if it gets dry (it should stay damp enough to stick together when you stick your finger into it, or when you push it into a little heap with your finger). Take care to add the water to the medium, *not* onto the eggs. The preferred humidity is 100 percent. Placing an open deli container, half filled with water, onto the hardware cloth shelf will also help maintain the humidity.

How do you know if the eggs are fertile or viable? Soon after laying, those eggs that are not fertile will turn yellow, harden, and begin to collapse. Should embryo death occur during incubation, discoloration follows. Fertile eggs will remain white and turgid to the touch. A week to a few days before hatching, fertile eggs may dimple. This is normal. Infertile eggs should be removed and discarded. Open the egg container daily after the 50th day of incubation to allow for air exchange.

At the end of the incubation period, which may vary in duration from 60 to 80 days, the baby iguanas will pip. The babies may remain in the pipped egg for as long as a day and a half. After they have hatched they should be moved to another terrarium and offered food, a sunning spot, and water. They should shed within a few days.

# Aggression and the Adult Iguana

There is one immutable fact about great green iguanas: if they are properly cared for, they grow. Females may attain a total length of 4–4.5 feet, males often grow to be 5.5–6 feet long and occasionally exceed 6.5 feet by an inch or two. These are *big* lizards. And no matter how much you like them, and how often you handle them, or how long you've had them, once they have attained sexual maturity, not all iguanas (especially males) remain tractable. They display especially unpredictable behavior during the breeding season. At this time, adult male iguanas may become *especially* aggressive toward a female owner. The need for careful approach and handling cannot be overemphasized. Castration is an option. It should be considered by iguana owners who do not wish to breed their pet or who are unable to contend with their iguana's mood swings.

Only a few years ago, neutering an iguana was very unusual. Today, with more knowledge about iguana behavior and with the increase in reptile oriented veterinarians, spaying/castration may be a consideration. It is not inexpensive, it is not entirely risk-free, nor is it a foolproof cure for aggressiveness, but it's one way owners of large iguanas can avoid becoming an iguana-bite statistic.

How much damage could an iguana actually do if it were to bite you? It depends, of course, on the size of the iguana and where it bites you. A severe bite by a 6-foot-long (up to 18 pounds!), hormone-driven male iguana on a hand, finger, throat, or face can be bloody and painful at best. Some bites can require reconstructive surgery. The bite by an adult female could be, but probably wouldn't be, nearly as bad. The jaws of these lizards are immensely powerful, and both jaws are liberally studded with sharp teeth. Remember that the surprise factor plays a part in the severity of the bite. Most iguana owners who have raised a 4-foot-long iguana from a hatchling have spent time taming their pet. The owner may place the

iguana atop its cage as usual while cleaning its cage. He or she doesn't expect that, when he or she returns with water dish in hand, Iggie will leap off its cage top, grab its owner's nose or fingers in its jaws, and twist.

Although female green iguanas are less apt to be as aggressively territorial when adult, spaying a female can have another benefit in addition to moderating behavior. It may prevent egg-binding (females bearing infertile eggs can have difficulty in laying them and become egg-bound as a result). This generally results in the death of the iguana unless the alert owner realizes what's going on and takes his or her iguana to the vet for an injection of oxytocin.

The degree to which castration will lessen the aggression problem seems to depend significantly on when it's done. If an adult male iguana is castrated at the height of his period of reproductive aggressiveness, his disposition may change little or not at all. On the other hand, if the castration occurs prior to sexual maturity, the iguana may never become aggressive. Only the owner—and his or her reptile vet—can decide the best course.

This large male iguana may become aggressive during breeding season.

# Special Interest Groups

## Herpetological Societies

Reptile and amphibian special interest groups exist in the form of clubs, monthly magazines, and professional societies, in addition to the herp expos and other commercial functions mentioned elsewhere.

Herpetological societies (or clubs) exist in major cities in North America, Europe, and other areas of the world. Most have monthly meetings, some publish newsletters, and many host or sponsor field trips and picnics or indulge in various other interactive functions. Among the members are enthusiasts of varying expertise. Information about these clubs can often be acquired by querying pet shop employees, high school science teachers, university biology department professors, or curators or employees at the department of herpetology at local museums and zoos. All such clubs welcome inquiries and new members.

Two of the professional herpetological societies are:

Society for the Study of Amphibians
    and Reptiles (SSAR)
Department of Zoology
Miami University
Oxford, OH 45056

Herpetologist's League
    c/o Texas National Heritage Program
Texas Parks and Wildlife Department
4200 Smith School Road
Austin, TX 78744

The SSAR publishes two quarterly journals: *Herpetological Review*, which contains husbandry, range extensions, news about ongoing field studies, and the like, and the *Journal of Herpetology*, which contains articles more oriented toward academic herpetology.

Hobbyist magazines that publish articles on all aspects of herpetology and herpetoculture (including lizards) are:

*Reptiles*
P. O. Box 6050
Mission Viejo, CA 92690

*Reptile and Amphibian Hobbyist*
Third and Union Avenues
Neptune City, NJ 07753

The hobbyist magazines also carry classified ads and news about herp expos.

The Internet contains a lot of information on reptiles in general and iguanas in particular. Use your search engine to find information about iguanas.

# Glossary

**Ambient temperature:** The temperature of the surrounding environment.

**Anterior:** Toward the front.

**Anus:** The external opening of the cloaca; the vent.

**Arboreal:** Tree-dwelling.

**Autotomize:** The ability to break easily or voluntarily cast off (and usually to regenerate) a part of the body. This is used with tail breakage in lizards.

**Caudal:** Pertaining to the tail.

**Cloaca:** The common chamber into which digestive, urinary, and reproductive systems empty and which itself opens exteriorly through the vent or anus.

**Crepuscular:** Active at dusk or dawn.

**Deposition:** As used here, the laying of the eggs.

**Deposition site:** The spot chosen by the female to lay her eggs.

**Dorsal:** Pertaining to the back; upper surface.

**Dorsolateral:** Pertaining to the upper sides.

**Dorsum:** The upper surface.

**Fracture planes:** Softer areas in the tail vertebrae that allow the tail to break easily if seized.

**Genus:** A taxonomic classification of a group of species having similar characteristics. The genus falls between the next higher designa-tion of family and the next lower designation of species. Genera is the plural of genus. The generic name is always capitalized when written.

**Gravid:** The reptilian equivalent of mammalian pregnancy.

**Hemipenes:** The dual copulatory organs of male lizards and snakes.

**Hemipenis:** The singular form of hemipenes.

**Juvenile:** A young or immature specimen.

**Lateral:** Pertaining to the side.

**Middorsal:** Pertaining to the middle of the back.

**Midventral:** Pertaining to the center of the belly or abdomen.

**Nocturnal:** Active at night.

**Oviparous:** Reproducing by means of eggs that hatch after laying.

**Poikilothermic:** A species with no internal body temperature regulation. The old term was cold-blooded.

**Posterior:** Toward the rear.

**Preanal pores:** A series of pores, often in the shape of an anteriorly directed chevron and located anterior to the anus.

**Saxicolous:** Rock-dwelling.

**Serrate:** Sawlike.

**Species:** A group of similar creatures that produce viable young when breeding. The taxonomic designation that falls beneath genus and above subspecies.

**Subcaudal:** Beneath the tail.

**Subdigital:** Beneath the toes.

**Subspecies:** The subdivision of a species. A race that may differ slightly in color, size, scalation, or other criteria.

**Terrestrial:** Land-dwelling.

**Thermoregulate:** To regulate (body) temperature by choosing a warmer or cooler environment.

**Tubercles:** Warty protuberances.

**Tympanum:** The external eardrum.

**Vent:** The external opening of the cloaca; the anus.

**Venter:** The underside of a creature; the belly.

**Ventral:** Pertaining to the undersurface or belly.

**Ventrolateral:** Pertaining to the sides of the venter (belly).

Note: Other scientific definitions are contained in the following two volumes:

Peters, James A. 1964. *Dictionary of Herpetology*. New York: Hafner Publishing Co.

Wareham, David C. 1993. *The Reptile and Amphibian Keeper's Dictionary*. London: Blandford.

# Index